Copyright 2021 Jacqualine Haller

All rights reserved.

ISBN: 9798738804434

After over a year long battle with ALS (Lou Gehrig's disease), my dear father was admitted to hospital January 2021. I left my home and drove halfway across Canada to be with him. We did not know how much time we had left.

I ended up being blessed with an additional 3 months by his side of incredible moments, visits with family and friends, and the many laughs and memories shared.

"Love you to the stars and back" was inspired by my family's true story, the story that unfolded in front of me while I shared these precious days with my father. I hope you enjoy reading it as much as I have enjoyed writing it.

~ Jacqualine Haller

Dedication

This book is dedicated to Grandpa John and Natalie.

A special thanks to Cheeko, the family Chihuahua

Thank you to my dear friend Monika for being my sounding board, and for the endless support in reading and re-reading the words on these pages. She is also a mother (the mother of my awesome godson Max) and was able to provide perspective on this special age group.

I have a Grandpa and a Grandma who are a lot of fun. They play with me at the playground. They help me down the slide and push me on the swing.

When they come to my house, we play with my toys together. When it is time to say goodbye, my Grandpa tells me he loves me to the stars and back. My Grandma tells me she loves me to the moon and back.

The stars and the moon seem far away in the sky.
They must love me a lot.
I love them very much too.

One day, when the weather outside was getting cooler and the leaves started to fall from the big tree in my yard, my Grandpa got tired and could not play with me as much as he used to. My Dad and Mom told me Grandpa got sick.

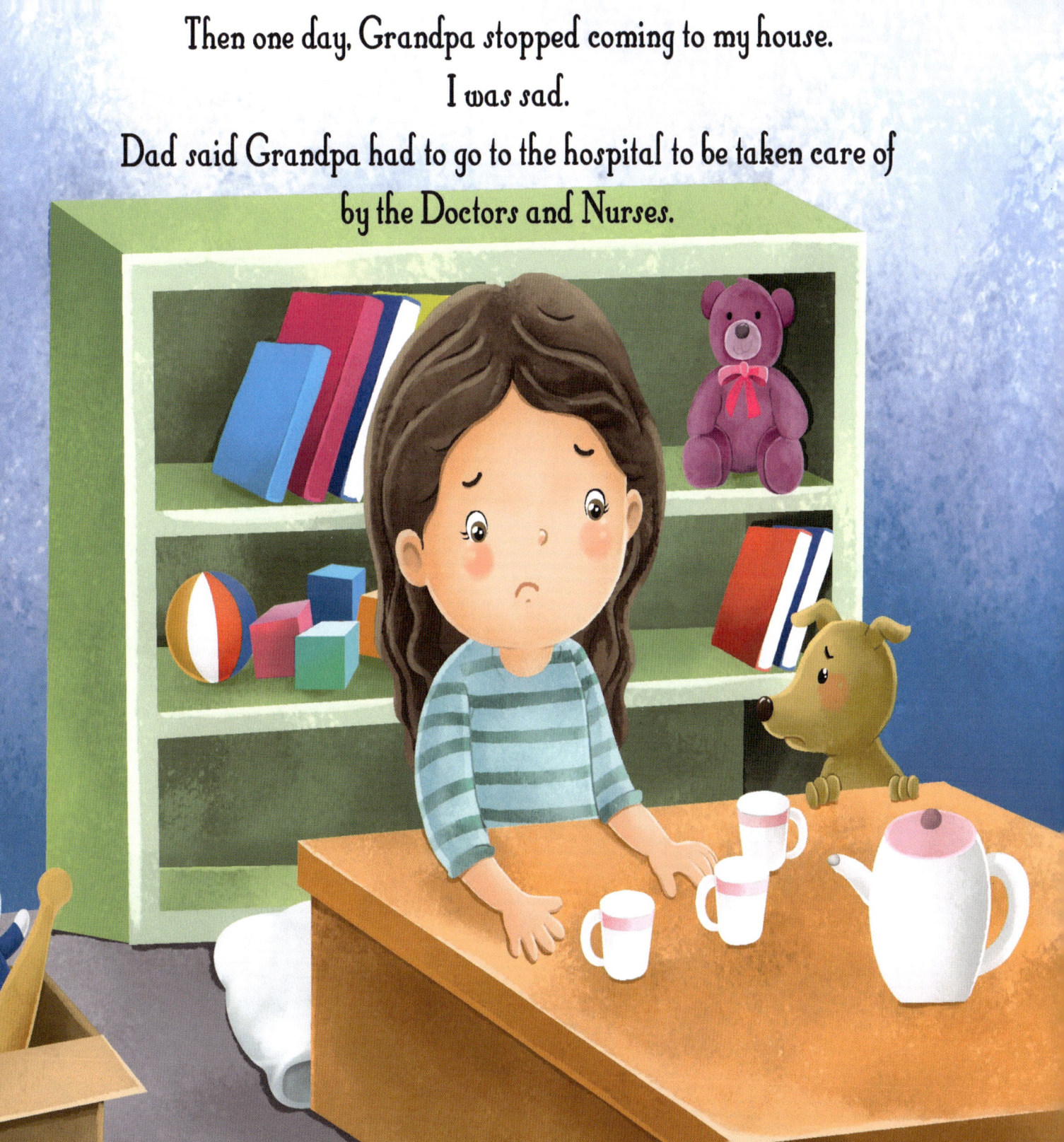

Then one day, Grandpa stopped coming to my house.
I was sad.
Dad said Grandpa had to go to the hospital to be taken care of by the Doctors and Nurses.

Sometimes, my Dad and Mom would let me come with them to visit my Grandpa. The Doctors and Nurses were very nice. They gave me juice and ice-cream.
I love my Grandpa

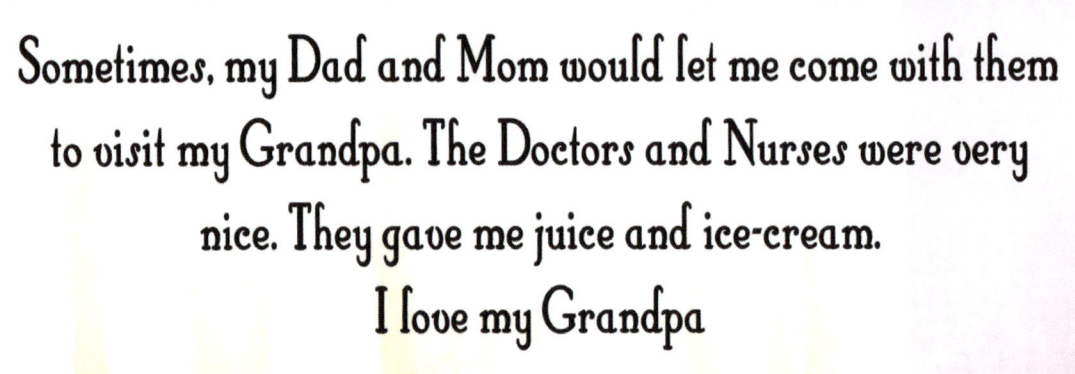

I had lots of fun looking at the stars and the moon with my Dad and Mom.
The globe and I became Best Friends. I took it everywhere I went.

Then, my Dad started to stay home more often. My Aunty came to visit from a big city.
There were Cousins and many people around.
Then, they all left.
My Dad told me that Grandpa became a star.

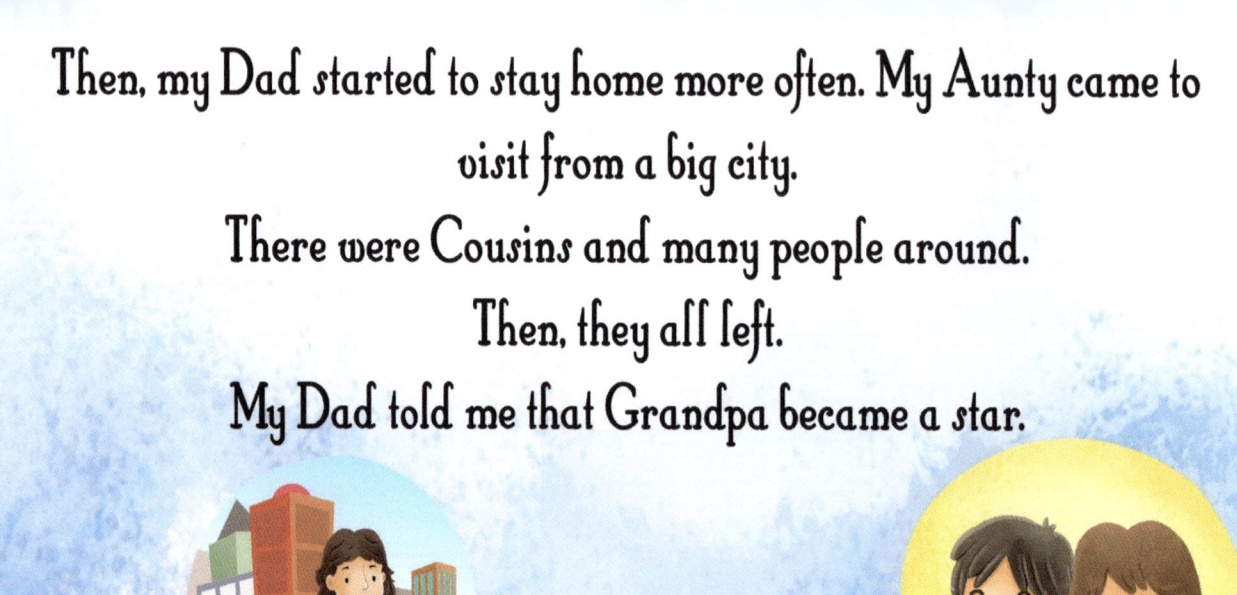

At first, I was sad I could not play at the playground with him anymore.
I was sad that he would not be there to help me down the slide and push me on the swing.
I missed my Grandpa.

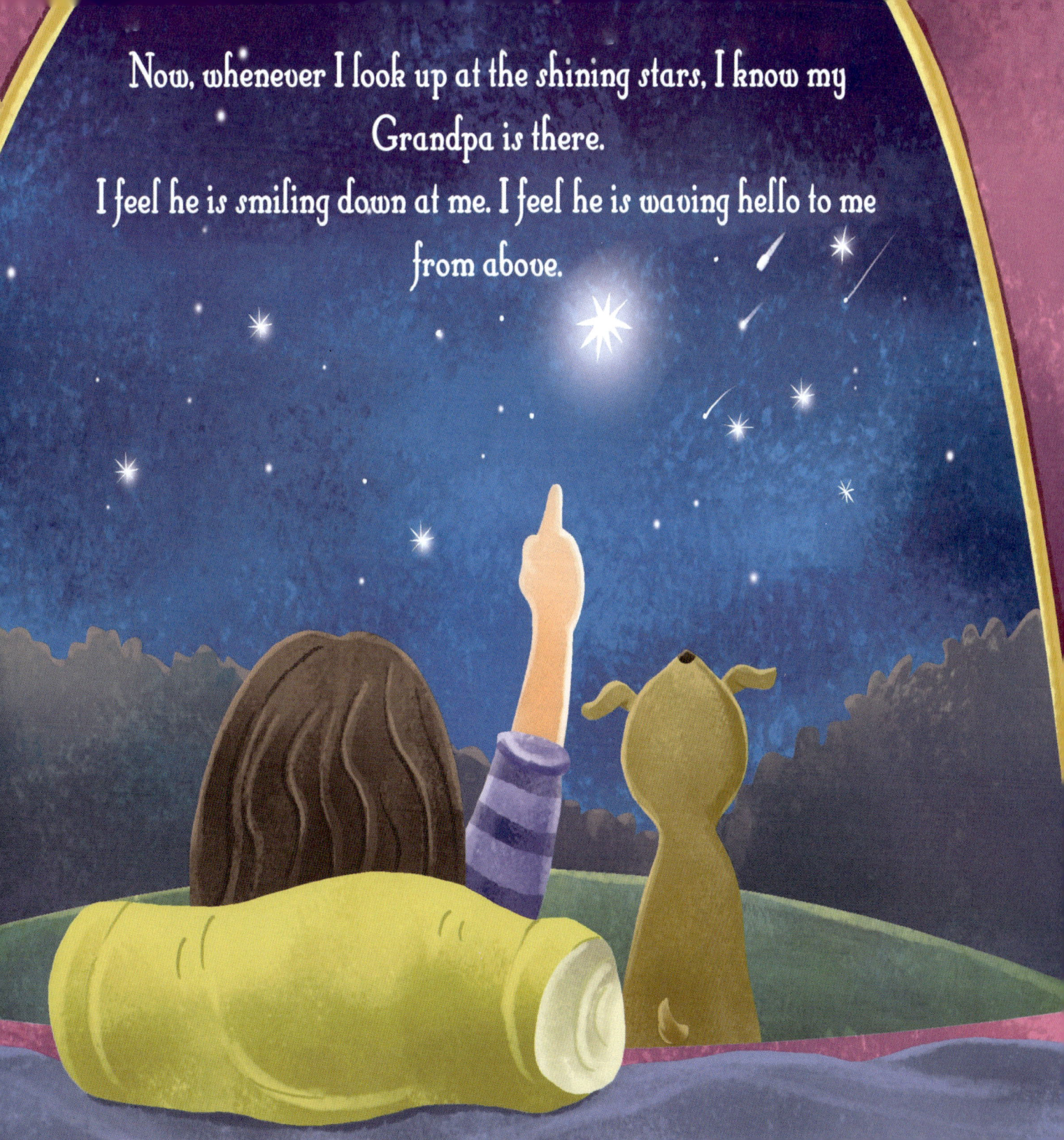

"Not the end♥"

Our family would like to extend our sincere gratitude to the incredible ALS team at the Saskatoon City Hospital for helping Grandpa John with his diagnosis.

Our deep appreciation is extended to the Palliative Care team at St. Paul's Hospital who provided exceptional care to him during the final stages of his illness.

Little Natalie and Grandpa John

Book Reviews

"I think your story was great! I loved your title and I think that the kids who read this will love the story. I also loved how the Grandpa says, " I love you too the stars and back." And I love how the Grandma says, "I love you to the moon and back." When the grandpa died, it was sad. When the granddaughter got the globe that shows stars, it reminded her of her Grandpa. It is special that she carried it around everywhere." - Sophia Smith, 10 years old

"Miss Jacqualine was working on the title and the ending of the story, which sounded very beautiful."
- Elijah Jellison, 7 years old

Georgia, 10 years old

Sienna Smith, 8 years old

Jack Smith, 7 years old

Mira Jellison, 3 years old

Thank you to all the children who provided their feedback for this book before it was published.

Mira, Sienna, Elijah, Jack, Sophia and Georgia
(left to right)

Miss Jacqualine & Grandpa John

Printed in Great Britain
by Amazon